ALMOST ADULT

ALMOST ADULT

CHARLOTTE ANNE-TILLEY

RENARD PRESS

RENARD PRESS LTD

124 City Road
London EC1V 2NX
United Kingdom
info@renardpress.com
020 8050 2928

www.renardpress.com

Almost Adult first published by Renard Press Ltd in 2023

Printed in the United Kingdom by Severn

ISBN: 978-1-80447-085-5

9 8 7 6 5 4 3 2 1

CONTENTS

ALMOST ADULT

To all my sisters from *that* workplace.

CHARACTERS

The actor multi-roles as all the characters.
When Hope's name is in bold, she is speaking to the audience.

HOPE

MUM

DAD

ANNABEL

JENNA

DAZ

BETH

EVA

SHARON

WAITRESS

PAULA

MIKE

HANNAH

KIT

LIZ

JIM

COSMO

INTERVIEWER

SCENE 1

HELLO LONDON

'Girls Just Wanna Have Fun' by Cyndi Lauper plays. HOPE *enters the stage dressed head to toe in London Underground merch and excitedly signals to her London Underground T-shirt, hat and socks. She introduces herself to a couple of audience members and asks them excitedly where they live.*

HOPE: Guess who moved to London this week? This bitch. Cuz I'm fearless.

(Slight pause. She beams at the audience.)

Bought this outfit at the Museum of London. Cool as hell. It's a kid's age eleven, but it fits like a glove. Three days in London, and I just can't bring myself to take it off. I wore it to Madame Tussauds, the London Eye and Magic Mike Live. Which, by the way, is actually quite scary. They thought I was part of a hen do. They got me on stage. I got very panicky. I guess I just don't like men's hips…

Anyway... London. Once I hit nineteen I finished college and worked at Tesco Metro for a year. It was quite clear to everyone, including me, I needed to get the hell out of suburban England. Mum was absolutely gutted.

MUM: Are you sure you want to move to London, Hope? It just seems such a shame when we've just painted your bedroom. And, I don't mean to be awful, but London? London. It's a very— The tube system is very confusing and complicated, you know. Do you remember when you forgot to get off the train in Macclesfield, and you ended up in Birmingham, and your Dad had to come and get you? And the National Rail is quite simple comparatively. Anyway, Macclesfield just got named the Most Improved Town in the North-West. Might be worth sticking around for a year or two, or three, even.

HOPE: For reference, my hometown, Macclesfield, is disgustingly boring. All my friends moved away, and there's nothing to do. (*Dead serious:*) It doesn't even have a crazy-golf course. On crazy-golf opportunity alone, London absolutely knocks it out of the goddamn park.

Dad, however, had other things on his mind.

HOPE: Dad, I'm going to live in London. Dad?

DAD: Oh, right, London. Yeah. Do my hands look like they've got bigger to you?

4

HOPE: And my fifteen-year-old sister Annabel was a massive sarcastic bitch about it.

ANNABEL (*sincerely*): How are you even going to find a flat in London? I hear the housing market is a shitshow and rent has hit a new high. Obviously, I'm fifteen, but I personally would prefer to go to York or Sheffield. Because I saw this thing on TikTok and it said, when you look at the quality of life and standard of living in London, in comparison with other cities, it's, comparatively, not worth it.

And London is just so middle class. I mean, obviously, I'm kinda middle class, but I sort of feel that I can observe the middle class from the outside, as well as being a part of it.

HOPE: I honestly have no idea what the hell she's talking about. Yes, I was on Spare Room eight hours a day, and yes, I got rejected an ungodly amount of times. (*Proudly:*) But my new housemate Jenna needed someone urgently for the box room with no window, and offered me the room over Facetime. (*She gives the audience a huge smile.*) So Annabel can shove her shitshow housing market up her ass as far as I'm concerned.

Jenna is, like, the most organised woman I've ever met. When I arrived with Mum, Dad and Annabel, the first thing she said to us was:

JENNA: Hi, Hope and family. It's 4 p.m.! I was expecting at 3! No bother. Follow me. sorry, do you mind taking your

5

shoes off? Gosh, those are dirty. What have you been doing? Did you go for a walk? In a forest? Is that why you were late?! Right, OK, there's dirt on the floor now, so I will have to vacuum that straight away, OK?

(JENNA *leaves to get the vacuum cleaner.*)

MUM (*compulsively*): You need to buy a carbon monoxide alarm. Or you'll die in your sleep.

HOPE: Ooh. What's carbon bonoxide?

MUM: Carbon *Mon*-ox-ide… Jesus Christ, Hope, I do worry. You don't *know* anything.

HOPE: I know loads of stuff.

MUM: God, seems like yesterday I was having you cut out of my stomach. And now you're moving to London – *London* of all places. Absolutely vile city. (*Lifts her legs for* JENNA *to vacuum.*) Sorry, Jenna.

JENNA (*vacuuming*): No, it's OK. I think it's a vile city too. Hah!

MUM: Well, there we go. I mean, the crime rates are shocking… knife crime, burglary, anti-social behaviour, sex trafficking, fraud, hate crime, modern slavery, murder, rape, sexual harassment, stalking, terrorism, bike theft… Oh, don't get me started on bicycles. Alan, has she told you she's getting a bike? Alan!

JENNA: Sorry, do you mind if I—

DAD: Oh, exercise, lovely.

MUM: It's not lovely, Alan. Are you not aware that cycling kills? Just think about it – don't make any rash decisions. And remember, we'll help you with one month's rent, and then you're on your own, OK.

HOPE (*annoyed*): Yes. I don't need your help.

MUM: So, good luck with your job interview. Like I said, smile, nod and, for crying out loud, don't wear that stupid T-shirt. Come on, you're nineteen years old. It's ridiculous—

HOPE: Mum, I wear what I want to wear. I'm a free-spirited independent woman now.

MUM: All right, OK, feminism… We do love you. You know that, don't you?

HOPE: Yeah. (*Suddenly embarrassed.*) I like you too.

HOPE: And, just like that, my adulthood began. I watched them drive down the road and disappear into the distance. (*Emotional:*) I didn't feel emotional at all.

SCENE 2

MEET DAZ

HOPE *does a physical comedy underground sequence to 'Going Underground' by The Clash. Before she sits, she puts on a blazer.*

HOPE: Job interview today. It's for a dinosaur-themed bar. Called Dinoworld. It's incredible. When you arrive, there's people in dinosaur costumes dancing in the windows. I feel high on drugs. I showed Mum the website. She said it looks over-stimulating. But I love over-stimulating stuff – I love dinosaurs and I love to party. So it's a dream come true, really... Oh, here's the manager.

(HOPE *reaches out for a handshake.*)

DAZ: Don't do handshakes – too formal. Cheers for waiting. Sorry, I was just designing a new cocktail. Thinking of calling it T. rex on the beach... Like sex on the beach... It's funny. There we go! Got there in the end.

8

So, I'm Daz. Man. Myth. Manager at Dinoworld. Ten years and counting. Got your CV here. You're from up north? That's a big tick. Manchester born and bred, me.

Great A level results. Oh shit, 2022 – you were the COVID generation. You didn't see your mates for like two years. Damn. Right, let's get this done. You worked at Tesco… (*He turns over the CV to see if there's anything on the back.*) And is that it? Or…?

HOPE: Erm, I used to volunteer at Guides… but I love dinosaurs. I think it's so sad that they all died, you know?

DAZ: Yeah, extinction is brutal, right?

HOPE: Yeah. But anyway…

DAZ: Yup, anyway… Dinoworld. What can I say? It's your average front-of-house immersive dinosaur bar customer experience role. And… Oh hang on, my phone's ringing.

Sorry, I'm doing a rap showcase tonight at The Crown. Do you know it? Come along if you want. Yeah, it's just the other half of my double act wants to practise. I'll… I'll… I'll call him back later.

So, there are a few departments: maintenance, entertainment and bar. As you can see, it's an intense job out there. Really hard work. You have to wear a

9

dinosaur costume all day, every day. Do you think you could handle that sort of commitment? We have to ask.

HOPE: Yeah.

DAZ: Great. I just have three rules. Be on time, be sound and don't under any circumstances mention *Jurassic Park*. You'll get sued. I can't stress that enough.

Right, well, you don't have much experience, but you're northern and you seem like a laugh. So why the hell not? Let's give you a shot.

HOPE: Thank you, Daz. You won't regret this.

DAZ: You just need to sign this… It's about making sure you don't spill the beans on the Dinoworld experience to potential customers.

(HOPE *has a quick scan and signs.*)

HOPE: OK. Financial independence here I come.

SCENE 3

FIRST DAY

HOPE *does a little dance with her newly acquired dinosaur costume (to 'Dinosaur' by Kesha).*

HOPE (*intense nervous energy*): First day today. I've been experimenting all morning with dinosaur face paint, and I've ironed my dinosaur costume three times. I'm gonna be the best dino Dinoworld has ever seen. When I arrive Daz is outside having a cigarette.

DAZ: Why've you got face paint on? This is serious work we're doing here. Don't take the piss, yeah?

HOPE: I head inside to the toilet and rub my face with wet toilet paper. (*To self:*) Don't know what I was thinking there.

When I come back out, the rest of my team have arrived. I scan the ground for potential boyfriends, but can't find anyone up to standard. Which is pretty goddamn annoying. I follow my team to the changing rooms and

11

am pretty surprised to learn that there are no cubicles. So I have to strip off in front of these strangers. Great.

I wish I wasn't wearing Disney underwear now.

I shuffle into a corner and try to conceal as much of my body as possible. I catch eyes with a girl wearing shorts under her jeans. Genius. The genius turns to me.

BETH: No budget for changing rooms, apparently. I'm Beth, by the way. Started here about two years ago, just after I moved down. Yeah. It's mostly southerners here, apart from Daz. I'll take you under my wing.

HOPE: Found my new best friend. Daz strides in…

DAZ: Sorry, sorry, sorry, yeah, I know, you're still getting changed, but we need to get started. I'm not looking. So, that's the new girl, Hope. She's only worked at Tesco before, so be gentle on her.

Right, notices, shout out to Mike, who called in a code black yesterday.

(DAZ *approaches* MIKE *as he gets changed. He puts his hand on* MIKE*'s shoulder.*)

(*Realising he's half naked:*) Ooh, OK. That woman probably would have died if it wasn't for you. Round of applause for Mike, please.

Which brings me to: make sure you know your codes. So, as I said, code black is a medical emergency. I remember it as *'Heart Attack? Code Black.'* Repeat that for me…

(*The audience repeats.*)

Good! And, code magenta. Terrorism. If terrorism is happening, we meet at the… (*He pauses.*) …The huge inflatable dinosaur. Come on, guys, I shouldn't have to keep reminding you. And code red is if any old men get handsy, yeah? And that radio call needs to go to security. Because that is not my job.

And final notice. I don't wanna tell you guys off. I'm a chill boss, as you know, but can we all please remember that you have to pay for food from the food trucks guys? If I hear of anyone else bribing catering for free burgers… there's gonna be trouble.

Right, rant over. OK, Jasmine, Mike and (*gesturing to* MIKE*'s penis*) the little fella, you're at the bar tonight. Hannah, Paula and Beth, you're our dancers. Liz, Eva and Jim, you're our entertainers. And… Kit and Hope, you are on toilet duty.

HOPE: Erm, toilet duty. That wasn't in the job description – there must be a mistake.

HOPE: Actually, Daz, I think I would nail the dancing in the windows. I've been practising. I know how to move. I think you should give me a shot.

DAZ: Ehm, I don't know. You've sort of got to work your way up to that, and you don't look like you can move.

HOPE: I can move.

BETH: Look, Daz, I'm feeling pretty tired today. I'll swap with Hope. Give her a go of the window dancing.

HOPE: Goddamn *legend*! I give Daz my sweetest smile.

DAZ: All right, show me what you're made of.

HOPE: Mission accepted. I take to the windows.

(HOPE *breaks out into an unbelievable improvised dance routine to 'London Bridge' by Fergie. She surprises herself.*)

HOPE: I dance. I clean. I work. Repeat. I climb the ranks at Dinoworld. Three weeks in, I'm landing window dancing three to four times a week. I impress everyone.

After one month at Dinoworld, Daz pulls me to one side.

DAZ: Well done, you've worked hard over the past few weeks. Keep up the good work, yeah.

HOPE: He rubs my shoulder… He says 'Keep up the good work' and he rubs my shoulder. That's not weird, is it? That's nice, I think.

HOPE: Thanks Daz, see you tomorrow.

SCENE 4

EMAIL HOME

HOPE: Dear Mum, Dad and Annabel,

I'm writing you an email because I am too busy to chat on the phone. Just wanted to say that things in London are pretty swell. Got the job at Dinoworld; it's magical – like Disney World, but better. And my manager loves me, so I think I'm probably gonna get promoted soon. Things are great with my housemate Jenna, too. I did, accidentally, leave a used period pad on the bathroom floor, but she was fine with it.

Dad, in response to your text, that's fine to redecorate my bedroom. I obviously don't need it any more.

Best wishes, kind regards and yours faithfully,

Hope

SCENE 5

DAZ IS IN A BAD MOOD

HOPE: Another day, another Dinoworld shift. I've been in London for six weeks now and, ball drop, being an adult isn't even that hard. I don't see what all the fuss is about. Seriously, guys, A levels were harder. I think I'm a more functional adult than most people here.

Kit dances around the place like a little kid, Hannah sucks up to Daz and Paula literally sucks her thumb. While I iron my dinosaur costume every day, even if it makes me late – I refuse to leave the house without an ironed dinosaur costume.

Seriously though, guys, everyone makes out that it's so hard to make money, but I just work six or seven shifts a week. Mike – Daz calls him small-dick Mike – he told me, because we're under London Living Wage, the best thing is to pick up as many shifts as possible. And I like being at Dinoworld all the time. It gets me out of the flat. Which is great. Because there's a mouse that also lives in my room, so I can create some boundaries there. I don't like agile animals. And yes, I am tired. I have never been more tired in my life! My eyes are so red, and the other day I fell asleep in the shower! But tiredness is 80% of what being an adult is. So I feel all the more mature for it. Not gonna lie, I would actually say that I'm probably more mature than Daz himself. I know he's the manager, but he can be a bit of a kid, no offence.

For example, he's in a bad mood right now. How do I know that? Well, he's pacing up and down and panting like a mad dog. Because, much like a five year old, he wants us all to know he's in a bad mood. And now he's calling us over. Brilliant.

DAZ: Right, listen up guys, sorry, excuse me. Can you take your fucking AirPods out, Kit? Right, I just need to say. It's not that hard to say hi to me when you arrive at work, yeah? I know I'm your manager and I'm high status, but I'm only human.

All I need is a quick 'How are you, Daz', 'How's your mental health, Daz?', 'Can I buy you a drink, Daz?' Will someone just ask me a question?! You, you… ask me a question, please?

(Audience member asks a question, and DAZ answers.)

Thank you! See, it's not hard. And you know what, I can't even remember the last time one of you gave me a hug. Now, I think that's pretty goddamn sad.

HOPE: I think that's the cue for one of us to give him a hug. He looks at me, and I avert my eyes. Mike reaches out and gives him a half-hearted pat on the shoulder. Oh dear.

DAZ: Cheers, Mike. Right, anyway, because of the lack of community spirit, I'm arranging a work night out. And I'm not saying it's compulsory because of 'legal' bullshit, but I'll be pretty goddamn disappointed if people don't turn up. So, let's just imagine, hypothetically, that it is compulsory, yeah? Jesus, don't look so horrified. There'll be a free bar tab. Oh, and it's glitter themed.

SCENE 6

WE MAKE COFFEE

HOPE: Two months of working at Dinoworld. Eight-hour shifts and we only get a twenty-minute break. Surely that's not legal? You'd get an hour and a half at Tesco on a good day.

But I'm making the most of my lunch break today. I'm spending it at this sophisticated independent café down the road. It's called We Make Coffee. Very cool. Very down to earth. Very London.

The woman in front of me just ordered a regular decaf oat caramel latté with cream, which I think sounds very mature, so I order exactly the same. Get myself a table in the window and check my emails like an adult. Don't have any, but at least I checked. What else do adults do in cafés? Maybe I need to buy a Kindle…

Just when I'm starting to feel restless, I spot my northern friend Beth.

HOPE (*standing, overexcited*): Beth! LEGEND!

BETH: All right mate!

HOPE: Isn't this great?

BETH: What?

HOPE: Just, London!

BETH: Oh, right, yeah...

HOPE: God, we're getting on like a house on fire.

HOPE: Thanks for giving me your window dancing position. That was really nice of you.

BETH: It's all right. I always feel a bit exposed up there anyway.

HOPE: You feel exposed? Why?

BETH: I think just sexy dancing to the streets of Shoreditch...

HOPE: I don't think it has to be sexy.

BETH: Oh, yeah, but Daz prefers it that way. For the brand.

HOPE: Hah, right... well, thanks, anyway. I enjoy it.

BETH: Shit, we better head back. We're gonna be late.

SCENE 7

YOU'RE LATE

HOPE: Beth and I arrive back five minutes late, along with Eva, the other nineteen-year-old. Daz is waiting outside for us.

DAZ: Welcome back.

BETH: Sorry, Daz, it's hard to get there and back in twenty minutes.

HOPE: Eva gently touches Daz on the forearm.

EVA: Aw, Daz, your hair looks great today.

DAZ: Does it? That's exactly what my mum said when I Facetimed her. Anyway, Beth, Tesco Kid…

HOPE: That's his new endearing nickname for me.

DAZ: This isn't the first time this has happened. Sort it out, yeah. Or there will be consequences.

21

HOPE: This is when my fatal flaw occurs to me. I have no time-management skills. I wake up. I tell myself I'll be early today. But I repeatedly get sucked into the vortex and find myself sprinting from Hoxton station time and time again. I've had to start getting creative with my excuses.

Sorry, my bus crashed into another bus and caused absolute anarchy. Sorry, I dropped an ice cream down myself and had to go back and get changed. Sorry, terrorist attack... I thought about copying Eva's tactics of telling him I like his hair. But I don't like his hair, and I can't bring myself to say it. But I'm definitely, definitely not going to be late tomorrow.

SCENE 8

VISIT FROM SHARON

HOPE: Sharon, the CEO of Dinoworld, is coming in today. We're all crowded into the meeting room, and she comes in wearing a pink two-piece suit with perfectly curled hair. She's a goddess.

SHARON: So, I've heard that some of you have decided it's now acceptable to take ridiculously long lunch breaks. Just so you know, you are entitled to twenty minutes per shift. K? If I keep hearing about twenty-five minutes or even thirty-minute lunch breaks... there's going to be warnings. And I will simply stop putting you on the rota. Look, I know you're on zero-hour contracts, but you have to take this job seriously, K? You guys know... I'm a busy, busy woman. I shouldn't have to come down here and tell you to get your act together.

(She gets up and squeezes DAZ*'s shoulder.)*

Daz is under enough stress as it is. Let's not leave him an understaffed team. Oh, and while I'm on it, we're understaffed tomorrow. I know you've got your work night out, but Dinoworld can't close because you're all hungover, K? I hope I can trust you to sort that out amongst yourselves. Daz.

DAZ: All right, everyone, to your positions.

HOPE: I can't help feeling like that was slightly aimed at me. I'm never ever gonna be late again.

SCENE 9

EMAIL TO MUM

HOPE: Dear Mum,

I'm not sure why you keep calling me. I've told you I am too busy. I had a really good day yesterday. I actually got… promoted at Dinoworld. Yeah, head of customer experience. So, yeah, that will be great for my CV. Cuz remember you were saying that it was scarce. So that's not a problem any more.

I just hope you've realised from me moving away that I am actually much more mature than you thought. It was quite clear that you all thought I would crash and burn. But I am thriving. I am a city girl through and through. Kind of embarrassing for you, really. But, yeah, I'll call you in a month or so.

Best wishes,

Hope

SCENE 10

GETS READY WITH BETH

HOPE: Beth and I are getting ready for the compulsory-
not-compulsory night out. We're running late. But yeah,
she invited me round to her house to get ready. Popular!
She queues a song...

BETH: Hope. Who's that on your phone screen?

HOPE: Oh, it's Timmy. Chalamet. It's Timothée Chalamet.

BETH: Right, so are you single then?

HOPE: Yeah, yeah, yeah, I'm single. Yeah... So, Sharon
seems—

BETH: Psychotic?

HOPE: I was gonna say, like a girlboss.

BETH: Oh yes, she's a girlboss and Daz is a nice young man.

HOPE: Hmm, yeah.

BETH: He's not a nice young man, Hope…

HOPE (*confused*): Yeah, yeah, I know… What has he done?

BETH: The general creepy vibe is the big thing and—

HOPE: You know what, I think we should head off. Wouldn't want to be late with my track record.

SCENE 11

CLUB

HOPE: Get to the club! Strobe lights. Cool. Beth grabs drinks. I grab a table. Check my phone, and I am confronted with Timothée Chalamet. Oh god, what was I thinking? I mean, I can't keep holding out for him. Guys, I don't even know him. Without a moment's delay, I change my home screen to a picture of myself – empowerment – and I download Hinge for good measure. I've been here two months now, and I still haven't found a boyfriend! It's getting silly. Right, let's have a quick swipe… Joe, 23: 'Sex with me. Nothing special. Won't change your life. But at least you can say you've done it.'

BETH: Dear god, Hope, don't swipe right for him.

HOPE *(puts her phone down on the table)*: I wasn't going to.

BETH: Look, Hope, hang on, stop swiping for a sec. I wanted to say sorry that Daz is giving you a hard time.

I don't think it's actually about the lateness, to be honest – it's rarely about what he says it's about...

Look, Daz, eh, Daz has favourites here. You might have picked up on that, I don't know, but I wanted to sit down and properly tell you what he's like and tell you what I've seen because—

DAZ: Surfing Hinge, ladies? You'll spot me if you're not careful.

HOPE: Great timing. I lock my phone. Without a second's delay, Daz sits between us.

BETH: All right, Daz. Thought you said there was a free bar tab?

DAZ: Oh, yeah, I made that up.

BETH: Course you did.

DAZ: Thank you so much for coming out, guys. It's great to see you two let your hair down. My northern girls. Honestly, I know I've been cracking down, but I think you two are great.

If we can spend some more time together and get to know each other as people then we could make it work for you at Dinoworld...

HOPE: Suddenly I feel a hand on my leg. He's stroking my leg.

I look over at Beth. I think his hand is on her leg too. Rubbing up and down. Under the table. Unseen. Rubbing.

We both sit there, frozen. Silent. Unable to move, speak or tell him to get the fuck off.

I guess this is what Beth meant when she called him a creep.

He lifts his hand to take a sip of his drink, and immediately, impulsively I shoot up from my seat.

I make a beeline for the toilet. I hide. I hide for nearly half an hour. It feels like the sensible thing to do.

SCENE 12

OUTSIDE THE CLUB

HOPE: When I come out, they aren't at the table any more. The bar is much quieter now. I head up the stairs and past security, and then I spot Beth with her phone in her hand, shivering.

BETH: Where did you go?

HOPE: Toilet.

BETH: For half an hour?

HOPE: Sorry… I felt pretty uncomfortable with that creep rubbing my leg. Like, seriously, what the hell was that about?

BETH: You did see he was rubbing my leg at the same time, didn't you?

HOPE: Yeah… you seemed like you had it under control.

(BETH *turns to leave.*)

Wait, no… I wasn't deliberately trying to… it was just like fight or flight or something. I just needed to get away for a second, because it was making me feel all… The way he was stroking me—

BETH: Seriously, would you shut the fuck up? You haven't got a clue, have you? I sat at the table waiting for you to come back, and you didn't… so I tried to hide on the dance floor so I didn't have to sit with him stroking my leg. And I don't know, out of nowhere he, like, lunged at me.

HOPE: Oh, shit.

BETH: That's not even… he grabbed my arse. He leaned in and told me he was going to fuck me. He tried to put his hand down my… down my…

HOPE: Jesus, I had no idea he was capable of that.

BETH: Of course he's capable of that, he's a fucking creep – that's what I've been trying to—

HOPE: I'm sorry.

BETH: No, don't do that – don't speak to me like I'm a victim.

HOPE: …What are you gonna do?

BETH: I don't know. Zero-hour contract. No other job to go to. Rent to pay. I haven't got a clue.

HOPE: ...Do you wanna go get a McDonalds?

BETH: And get a Happy Meal? No, Hope. I'll see you at work.

SCENE 13

WASH YOUR DISHES

HOPE: McDonalds in hand, I arrive home to find my housemate Jenna is sitting on the sofa staring at me. What. The. Hell.

HOPE: Holy— Jenna, you scared the crap out of me—

JENNA: Yeah. Soo… I was just trying to work out if those are your dishes or mine… They're yours. All of them: the pans and the bowls, and the plates, and the mugs.

HOPE: Right. Isn't it like 2 a.m.?

JENNA: Yes, it is, Hope.

HOPE: She whips out a sponge and bottle of washing-up liquid from her jacket pocket. That's a bit odd, isn't it?

JENNA: Do you mind? Thanks. I'll be in my room.

HOPE: She's quite intense, isn't she? I walk over to the dishes and rinse my Timothée Chalamet mug. (*She starts doing the dishes, feeling almost emotional.*) Jesus Christ, this is boring. I don't want to waste my life washing dishes, man. There are so many. And the problem is the food has, like, stuck to them now. It's impossible.

As I place Timmy in the drying rack my phone buzzes... Oh my god. I got a match on Hinge. And it's my favourite guy so far. He's called Cosmo. He rides a skateboard. And he's twenty-three, so he must be mature. Wow. I never thought Cosmo would swipe back for me.

Holy crap, he's messaged me: 'So, date, next Thursday?'

Maybe. Maybe. Maybe everything's gonna be OK now? The dishes can wait.

SCENE 14

RESEARCHES HARASSMENT

'Therefore I Am' by Billie Eilish plays.

HOPE: I'm researching sexual harassment. I need to know about this shit. Apparently. Definition: unwanted behaviour of a sexual nature. Is a leg rub sexual? Maybe a leg rub could be friendly. A friendly leg rub. But then there's the weird comments, and how he always comes in when we're getting changed. That does feel…

Thing is, when you think about it… what he did to Beth was categorically bad. On paper, it would sound bad. Like, actual proper sexual harassment. A leg rub just doesn't have the same 'oh my god, what a terrible boss' vibe to it. It's more 'that's weird, I guess'.

I mean, obviously I don't want him to touch me at all, but it was my leg. Not my boob.

So in a strange way, I should kind of be grateful for that.

SCENE 15

WHERE DID YOU GO

LAST NIGHT?

HOPE: There's a weird atmosphere at Dinoworld today. I told a few people in the changing room what Daz did to Beth, and I don't quite get the outrage I'm expecting. Beth pulls me to one side.

BETH: Can you stop telling people what happened?

HOPE: Yeah, sure.

HOPE: Oops… Daz stumbles into our changing room unshaven and slightly sweaty. My pelvic floor actually tenses at the sight of him. Jesus, if that isn't fight-or-flight I don't know what is.

I stare at the floor for the duration of the briefing.

DAZ: Uh, Hope and Eva, yeah, you're gonna be on toilet duty tonight.

HOPE: I wonder what Eva did wrong. I sneak a look at him and discover he is, in fact, walking towards me. Oh no…

Here he comes and he's here. He's here.

DAZ: So where did you disappear off to last night? You got up and left. Bit fucking rude, mate.

HOPE: I just really needed the toilet. I, erm, have a bladder infection.

DAZ: Well next time wait till I've finished talking, like an adult. You're gonna have to play ball if you want to go back to dancing in the windows.

SCENE 16

EVA IN TOILETS

HOPE: Toilet duty. It's, essentially, just standing outside the toilets. That's literally it. Then checking that no one's been throwing toilet roll all over the floor or pooing up the walls – that sort of thing. Safe to say I prefer dancing in the windows.

I've been standing here at least two hours now, and I feel all light-headed and woozy. And, I don't mean to be dramatic, but it feels like my chest is about to explode, and my breathing has gone all weird. Yeah, OK, no, I need to take a second…

(*She locks herself in one of the cubicles and tries to control her breathing.*)

Oh god. Oh god. I don't know why I'm so… I feel bad.

A knock on the door. Oh no, has Daz come into the women's toilets?

EVA: Hope, are you all right in there?

HOPE: It takes me a second. And then I realise it's Eva. Daz's favourite. The one he drives home after work. He's borderline obsessed with her. The one who always compliments his hair.

HOPE (*opening the door*): Yeah, I'm fine, just needed to... wee.

EVA: Is he being... difficult? ...Look, Hope, I know what he is. Some of the girls don't, but I do. He's a predatory piece of shit and, full disclosure, we're taking him down.

HOPE: Holy crap, she's a boss.

EVA: I've spoken to Beth. She told me what happened the other night. She's not the only one. There are tens of women he's done this to. Some of them you haven't even met. They quit before you started.

HOPE: But I thought you—

EVA: Yeah, I tried playing his game, getting ahead. But I'm done. It's time to take him down.

HOPE: So are you going to speak to HR?

EVA: Dinoworld doesn't have an HR department. And we signed NDAs when he started, so it's all a bit—

HOPE: Damn, I should've read what that was.

EVA: We're going to head office to speak to Sharon. Beth took a bit of convincing, but she's in. Write a statement and have it ready. This is war.

SCENE 17

MEETING WITH SHARON

HOPE: Dinoworld's head office is so posh. They have a ping-pong table in the foyer. And a free fizzy-drinks machine. So far I've had a Coke and a Sprite. I'm feeling pretty reckless...

The waiting room is filled with boss-ass women who are tired of Dinoworld's bullshit. I smile across at Beth. She gives me a thumbs up. I love her. At 10 a.m. on the dot, Sharon emerges from one of the offices. Her hair is perfectly curled.

SHARON: Hope? Would you like to follow me?

HOPE: I follow her down the corridor, cool as a cucumber.

SHARON: OK, so I want to start by saying that predatory behaviour is *unacceptable* and absolutely not tolerated at Dinoworld. So, in your own time, can you tell me what happened to you?

HOPE: Sure, Daz rubbed my leg—

SHARON: You are joking? That's *horrific*.

HOPE: Well, I know it's not *horrific*. Like, I know that it could be worse…

SHARON: Oh, so you wouldn't say that it's that bad. That's interesting.

HOPE: No, I do think it's bad.

SHARON: Right, and did he keep doing it even when you told him to stop? …You did tell him to stop?

(*Slight pause.*)

HOPE: …I'm not sure. But it wasn't just the leg thing anyway – there's also, like, shoulder rubs, creepy staring and, like, manipulation.

SHARON: What do you mean by manipulation?

HOPE: Like, he always puts his favourites in good positions.

SHARON: I'm sure we're all guilty of that!

HOPE: It's not… It's hard to… He assaulted my friend too. She's outside.

SHARON: I see. Is she the one that encouraged you to come in today?

43

HOPE: No, that was Eva—

SHARON (*makes a note in her notebook*): OK, Eva. Great. OK.

HOPE: But, yeah, what he did to Beth was really bad – you'll see.

SHARON: I'm sure I will. So I think that's all I need. And just so you know, we're a small team, and we don't have anyone to cover Daz. So he'll be continuing his role while the investigation is ongoing.

HOPE: Erm, oh right, really? So, he's in tomorrow. Cool, cool.

SHARON: All right, thank you, Hope.

HOPE: No, thank you.

HOPE: Well, I feel like overall I kind of smashed that.

SCENE 18

DATE

HOPE *gets changed to 'Man! I Feel Like a Woman' by Shania Twain. She dances around trying to hype herself up.*

HOPE: I've got my date with Cosmo tonight. After hours of preparation, I'm very pleased with the final product. I look amazing.

I walk down the road to the absolute admiration of the people I pass along the way. Seriously, I get catcalled three times. Which is disgusting, but at least I know I look good.

He's suggested this incredible ball-pit bar. I'm obsessed. It's better than Dinoworld. I grab us a table by the ball pit. Can't wait to dive in there later. Cheeky.

I sip a rainbow cocktail and wait. I think Cosmo's running late...

I text him. No reply.

I call him. His phone's off. Ahh…

I look up to see a middle-aged man making his way towards me with Daz eyes. No. No. Please don't. He makes some disgusting comment, and I find myself running to the toilets. Third time this week.

SCENE 19

ASKS FOR ANGELA

HOPE: I'm not stupid, by the way.

I know I've been stood up. I know my housemate hates me. I know that working at Dinoworld is really, really bad for my mental health, and I did a pretty shit job of explaining that in my meeting with Sharon.

I don't want you to think I don't know all those things. Because I do know. I just really wanted this to be good.

(*She looks down for a moment, then looks up again.*)

I look up from the floor to see a sign on the door. It says, 'Ask for Angela. Feel like you're in an unsafe situation? Ask the bar for Angela, and we'll get you home.'

OK.

As I open the toilet door, I see a woman in a work uniform applying lipstick.

WAITRESS: Are you OK, love?

HOPE: Can I have Angela please?

WAITRESS: Yeah, I'll call you a taxi…

HOPE: It's just that—

WAITRESS: You don't need to explain.

(*Turns to leave, and then:*) Sorry, men can be idiots.

(HOPE *gives her a small smile.*)

SCENE 20

SOLIDARITY

HOPE: I slip silently into my taxi and am home within five minutes. When I arrive home, Jenna's watching *Made in Chelsea*.

JENNA: Everything OK?

HOPE: Ehm, I'm having a bit of a tricky day.

JENNA: With?

HOPE: Men keep… My boss is a predator. I got stood up and this creepy man at the bar started, you know.

HOPE: She pauses *Made in Chelsea*.

JENNA: I'm sorry.

HOPE: I thought things had been getting better. Everyone's always talking about the fact that it's got better.

JENNA: No, things are still pretty bleak.

HOPE: I'm realising that. I have to see my boss at work tomorrow.

JENNA: He hasn't been suspended? Right.

(*Slight pause.*)

JENNA: Look, Hope, you did a good thing. You spoke out. That's all we can ever do, isn't it? And the reality is the investigation will end soon, and it will all be over.

HOPE: Yeah, you're right… and, Jenna, sorry I'm rubbish at being a housemate.

JENNA: It's OK.

SCENE 21

CORNERED AT WORK

There is another sequence of HOPE *going on the London Underground. 'The Fear' by Lily Allen plays.* HOPE *is now more anxious and understated.*

HOPE: I arrive twenty-five minutes late, cuz I don't care.

Outside Dinoworld Hannah, Paula and Mike are smoking. I eavesdrop as I come up behind them.

PAULA: I just think he's a bit of a man child.

MIKE: Yeah, like *me*. I'm a man child. He's never tried anything with me either. I think he's just a bit socially awkward.

HANNAH: Well, yeah, thing is I just think we need to…

It's unfair – like, he hasn't really done anything that bad. He's not creepier than men generally are. I think it's all a bit dramatic.

51

Like, at this point, I kind of think we need to say something, cuz it's just one narrative being spread around, you know.

PAULA: Yeah, maybe.

HOPE: They fall silent as I pass. Oh, and yeah, Hannah is American. She came all the way to London to work at Dinoworld. Sad.

I get to the changing room and it's empty. Finally, some privacy.

(*She starts getting changed.*)

I hear the door open… It's Daz.

(*She quickly puts her top back on.* DAZ *sits for quite some time.*)

DAZ: Have you heard about this witch-hunt? People going to head office about me?

Hilarious. It's actually really funny.

…Apparently you were there. I was a bit shocked by that. Cuz I feel like I took you under my wing and that. I gave you a job when you had fuck-all experience, didn't I? Out of the kindness of my heart. So, yeah.

(*He pauses, strategising.*)

It was the leg rub, right? You didn't like me rubbing your leg.

A leg rub. And I could lose my job. Nah... I don't think one person's issues with physical contact should put another person out of work.

Hannah doesn't mind me rubbing her leg. Paula doesn't mind. So clearly I'm not the problem. That's all I'm saying. That's literally all I'm saying...

HOPE: ...You know what, Daz? I think you are a really, really terrible person. And your breath stinks.

(*Mic drop moment...* HOPE *walks out.*)

HOPE: I think about throwing a rock at Daz's car on the way out. But that would be immature.

SCENE 22

EMAIL FROM SHARON

SHARON: Good Afternoon Hope,

I write to inform you of the outcome of the recent investigation. Given the nature of the grievance, we have decided to conduct a thorough investigation to satisfy ourselves that we are running a safe workspace. But please note that we are actually not obliged to hear grievances from our zero-hour staff.

I carefully considered the evidence gathered from the investigation. A number of people have come forward, both in support of Darren Smith and against, so I hope you appreciate it has not been easy to reach a fair and balanced decision on the basis of such conflicting opinions.

Based on my view of the various statements and conversations, I am of the opinion that some of the complaints raised were, in part, unfounded, and relate more to the management style of the individual involved.

The majority of the issues would not have escalated and could have been dealt with in a timely manner if people had come forward earlier. If you feel uncomfortable with a situation or feel that your boundaries are not being respected, you have a responsibility to raise that.

Since the investigation has taken place, Darren Smith has tendered his notice of resignation and will not be returning to site. We would also advise that you seek employment elsewhere, so that we can have a fresh start at Dinoworld free from hostility and resentment.

Many thanks,

Sharon

SCENE 23

MUM PHONE CALL

We hear the beep-beeps of a phone ring out.

HOPE: Mum?

MUM: Hope, it's lovely to hear from you… Is everything OK?

HOPE: I'm sorry.

MUM: What is it?

HOPE: I… I've lost my job.

MUM: How did that happen?

HOPE: I tried to do the right thing – I tried to help my friend and… (*She sighs.*)

MUM: What did we say about keeping your head down?

HOPE (*hurt*): Mum! That's not… my manager assaulted my friend, and we both lost our jobs because the boss took his side. OK?

MUM: Right, oh gosh.

(*Pause.*)

HOPE: I just… how did this happen? How did the world become so bleak and disappointing?

MUM: Is this why you haven't called? Your dad and I have been really worried about you.

HOPE: I did email.

MUM: I know.

HOPE: …It sounds so obvious, but I realised the other day that I'm, like, never going to be a kid again.

Don't you think that's horrible?

MUM: But you were ready to move out, weren't you, Hope?

HOPE: Yeah, I used to moan, but Macclesfield's my home, isn't it?

I don't know if London will ever be my home. Life is lived so differently here. I don't know how to sit. I don't know how to talk to people. I don't know how to dress.

I don't know what to do. What should I do? Do you…
do you think I should come home? Can I come back to
Macclesfield, do you think?

MUM (*exhaling*): Of course you can. Macclesfield will always
be your home. It's been hard, I can see that. But it will
get easier. Everyone feels lost for a little while. You're
certainly not on your own.

I think, if you stick it out, you could be very happy in
London.

HOPE: Yeah, I think I should give it one last shot…

It's been hard though, Mum. Harder than I ever thought
it would be.

MUM: I am sorry… We do love you. You do know that, don't
you?

HOPE: Yes. I love you too.

SCENE 24

GOODBYE BETH

HOPE: It's been a few weeks since I got fired and I'm seeing Beth for the first time since.

We walk around Green Park. I've been doing a lot of that recently. Walking, lying under trees, mindful stuff. After a couple of hours we arrive at Green Park station, and Beth turns to me.

BETH: All right, this is it.

HOPE: Yeah… Beth, I wanted to— I can't help feeling like it was, kind of, my fault. I didn't explain it right. And I sort of said you guys pushed me into doing it.

BETH: Don't beat yourself up. Maybe you didn't nail it, but we were never going to win anyway.

HOPE: You know, we could go to the press? We could try and do something big about this?

BETH: I don't think I can, Hope. I need to get away from it all now.

HOPE: Yeah, I get that.

BETH: I'm gonna go back up north. I probably won't see you for a while. But good luck with everything, yeah. I really, really wish you the best.

SCENE 25

NEW JOB

'Skinny Love' by Bon Iver plays. HOPE *folds her dinosaur costume and packs it up into a box. She puts on her blazer.*

HOPE: I've got a job interview today. You won't believe where it's for – We Make Coffee. It's not flashy or particularly exciting. But I think I could float along nicely here…

I think I could manage.

INTERVIEWER: Would you like to come through?

HOPE: Yes.

(She shares a moment with the audience before leaving the stage.)

ACKNOWLEDGEMENTS

Almost Adult has been part of my life since 2019, and there are a lot of people who I have worked with along the way who have helped to shape the play. The show began as a thirty-minute zoom play. Before it ever saw the light of day, I shared it with my wonderful friend (and talented actor) Georgia Cudby, who gave me all the insight and motivation I needed to keep writing. Thank you, Georgia.

The thirty-minute zoom play (which was filmed during the COVID pandemic) was featured in the Command Fringe Festival and Online@theSpaceUK. Harry McMullen played Daz/Dad, Jessica Parsons played Mum, Fiona Townsley played Annabel, Zoë Birkbeck played Beth and I played Hope. The cast opened my eyes to how much I could do with each of these characters, and each of their interpretations still lives within the solo show. This production was directed by Kate Somerton. Kate is a patient and thoughtful director, who allowed each of us to work in our own creative ways. Thank you also to Zoë for photographing *Almost Adult* at several stages of its development. (See cover for reference!)

In 2021, *Almost Adult* (the solo show) was born. During this time, myself and Imogen Mackie Walker (the assistant director of London productions at the Old Red Lion

Theatre and The Space Arts Centre) interviewed around twenty people about their experiences of workplace sexual harassment, as well as their experience living in a city. I found these interviews profound and moving. However, they also lit a fire within me. I saw myself in each of them, and I applaud them for their bravery in engaging in a conversation that is tough and much easier to avoid.

I teamed up with Imogen Mackie Walker and Beth Wilson for a year of collaborating on *Almost Adult*. Working with Imogen and Beth was a truly fulfilling process. We devised, we discussed and they took lots of photos of me in my London Underground outfit at Winter Wonderland. Imogen and Beth are inquisitive creatives, and they were the perfect collaborators for this stage in the process when we were still getting to know Hope and the other characters that inhabit this world. Thank you also to the Old Red Lion Theatre and The Space Arts Centre for hosting *Almost Adult*, and to all the audience members who came along. I am particularly thankful to Inquisitive Pictures film-makers Linda Ludwig and James Curle, who came to see *Almost Adult* during this time and have been so instrumental in helping me to grow as both an actor and a writer. I wouldn't be where I am now without their guidance and wisdom.

August 2022! While Imogen delved into the world of screen acting and Beth began to soar in the queer theatre scene, I headed up to Edinburgh with resident director Lorna McCoid, resident movement director Evie Appleson and production assistant Carmel Skinner. Getting a fresh pair of eyes on the show was brilliant, and we spent four days honing the play in preparation for Edinburgh Fringe. Here's to Lorna, Evie and Carmel for all the hard work they put in to tackling the beast that is Fringe.

And gosh, where to start with Edinburgh Fringe? It was a wild month, and I felt lucky to be at the glorious female-run venue, Gilded Balloon. Karen and Katy Koren, who run Gilded Balloon, are at the forefront of championing funny women in both theatre and comedy, and it was a joy to perform at their space. One of the most special things about Edinburgh Fringe was the host of incredible female and non-binary creatives I met while I was up there. In particular, Kylie Vincent, Olivia McLeod, Mabel Thomas and the SoLaFlair team became wonderful friends. We supported each other through the month, and I am so grateful to have met them.

That brings us to 2023. I am returning to Ed. Fringe with a new version of *Almost Adult*. The team has expanded this year to include Elf Lyons (comedy advisor), PJ Cunningham (assistant producer), Chloé Nelkin Consulting (publicists), Steph Parry and Olivia McLeod (acting advisors).

Elf, Steph and Olivia have pushed me to make the show the best it possibly can be. And I am hugely grateful to them for investing their time and energy into taking the show to the next level. PJ has been the queen in shining armour, putting out fires and offering wisdom in our long zoom calls. Similarly, Chloé and the team at CNC have been a game changer in putting *Almost Adult* on the map, and we continue to be in awe of their all-female team. Ugly Duck Theatre and the Bridge House Theatre have also been fabulous allies during this year's rehearsal process.

We are also working with The Survivor's Trust this year, who are an incredible trust. They offer support and guidance to survivors of sexual violence, and they have been providing us with resources and advice for audiences on workplace sexual harassment.

And thank you to Will at Renard Press for believing in *Almost Adult* and putting my work in print for the first time. It takes people like Will to nurture emerging playwrights, and he has been brilliant to work with throughout the publishing process.

And of course, I have to thank my family for supporting my ambitions and for seeing the show a crazy amount of times. My mum has always been at the other end of the phone for the highs and the lows of this process (and of life), and I am so grateful to have her as my mum.

And finally, thank you to *you* for buying this play.